POETRY OF LEADERSHIP
AND COMPASSION

PROFESSOR PATRICK PIETRONI

FRESCO BOOKS

CONTENTS

INTRODUCTION

The first six volumes of this series covered:

The framework of these short volumes allows the reader to have an introduction to the specific focus of the book. They are accompanied by poems and images that help to add an aesthetic and emotional experience.

This final volume covers, and probably most importantly, explores the concept of leadership. In October 2015 we launched the Darwin International Institute for the Study of Compassion, which was to be supported by the charity, the Darwin Center Trust. During the conference I was interviewed for the *Huffington Post*, and in the subsequent publication the article was labelled, "Something Has to Change in Today's World! Let's Start with Future Leaders From Across the Globe".[1]

As I write this volume on leadership we have witnessed two very different styles of leadership in the election for the next President of the United States. Each of the candidates secured over 70 million votes. So, notwithstanding their political differences as candidates for the most powerful leadership post in the world, they communicated two very different models of leadership. When we launched the Darwin International Institute for the Study of Compassion we were wanting to provide a scholarship programme, much like the Fulbright or Rhodes scholarships, to ensure that our future leaders, whether in commerce, business, healthcare, education or engineering, etc. understood what compassion means, what undermines it and how it can be fostered by individuals, organisations and society. My colleague, Mohamed Keshavjee (an International cross-cultural specialist in mediation), wrote in the Ismaili Mail:

> *Some may wonder where Charles Darwin fits into all of this. Contrary to popular belief, Darwin was not responsible for the glib shorthand of "survival of the fittest" which is so often applied to his theory of evolution in natural selection. In his three major works – On the Origin of Species, The Expression of the Emotions in Man and Animals, and The Descent of Man – it is possible to trace his understanding of the evolutionary nature of compassion and empathy, although he refers to these qualities in terms of "sympathy", "moral actions" and "social instinct" in keeping with contemporary Victorian terminology. In many ways, Darwin's position appears to reject the primacy of crass self-interest, focusing instead on a range of human emotions, including sympathy for others, including those beyond our family group or species. In The Descent of Man, Darwin wrote: "We are …*

impelled to relieve the sufferings of another, in order that our own painful feelings may be at the same time relieved. In like manner we are led to participate in the pleasure of others".

In short, Darwin's research suggests that humans have evolved to behave compassionately, or at least that we have the capacity to do so. Recent discoveries in neuroscience and neural-imaging support this biological basi for compassion, but it was Darwin who originally argued that "those communities which contained the greatest number of the most sympathetic members would flourish best, and rear the greatest number of offspring". In support of continuing Darwin's legacy, his great–great-granddaughter, award-winning British poet, author and scholar, Professor Ruth Padel, is Patron of the Darwin Centre Trust.[2]

So, in this last volume in the series we bring together the three recurrent themes of the previous volumes: poetry, leadership and compassion. It is fair to say in this introduction that the literature available on leadership and compassion could fill two libraries, and it is also true to say that almost all the various academic disciplines will have a different approach at trying to describe what is meant by these two terms.

LEADERSHIP

The call to lead is spiritual
starting with the noble appointment
and courageous display of trust
by those who anointed you
entrusting their project to you
enshrining their confidence in you
Assigning their powers to you
With the wealth of their purse
Dressing your ego
magnifying your image
in a portrait of great leaders
engraving your name
among the list of supreme leaders
in a daylight display of the human Spirit.

Kenneth Maswabi [3]

TYPES OF LEADERS

In his book How to Lead [4] Rubenstein chooses the following types of leadership and gives explanations and descriptions using living examples:

Visionaries – Bill Gates, Sir Richard Branson
Builders – Ken Griffin, Marilyn Hewson
Transformers – Melinda Gates, Indra Nooy
Commanders – General Colin Powell, Condoleezza Rice
Decision Makers – Dr Anthony Fauci, Justice Ruth Bader Ginsburg
Masters – Jack Nicklaus, Renée Fleming

He also looks back on his own career and identifies the *"attributes that enabled me to go from something of a non-leader in my first phase of life to a leader in the second and third."* [5] These were:

luck; desire to succeed; pursuit of something new and unique; hard work; long hours; focus; failure; persistence; persuasiveness; humble demeanour; credit sharing; ability to keep learning; integrity; responding to crises.

The literature on leadership is overwhelmed with lists such as this and I have chosen some of my favourite to illustrate quite how complex and diffuse the concept of leadership has become. I start with a simple outline of different styles of leadership and the difference between what action leaders and process leaders bring to their work. Clearly a leader can be both top-down and bottom-up, and will be guided by what he/she considers to produce the best outcome.

LEADERSHIP AND MANAGEMENT

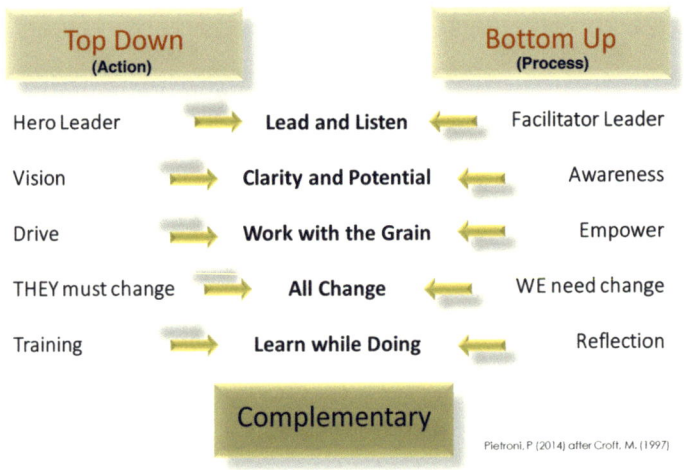

Leadership Styles

Top Down (Action)	Lead and Listen	Bottom Up (Process)
Hero Leader	Lead and Listen	Facilitator Leader
Vision	Clarity and Potential	Awareness
Drive	Work with the Grain	Empower
THEY must change	All Change	WE need change
Training	Learn while Doing	Reflection

Complementary

Pietroni, P (2014) after Croft, M. (1997)

A GOOD LEADERSHIP

A good leader
leading by example
is a good leader
showing the way
By rational moves
with endurances and love
He rules his subjects
Disciplines of people
He make his goals
The subject progress is
All his dream
Education, A must
To good leader
As ass on the throne
Formal education not only his yard stick
With life's experience
A good leader, A jewel
At home
write by james.

James Prince [6]

A "leader" may not be a very good manager, and vice versa a manager may not be a good leader. The next table attempts to compare and contrast the difference between the two.

Leadership complements management; it doesn't replace it.

Good management brings a degree of order and consistency.

Leadership is about coping with change.

Management starts by planning and budgeting.

Leadership starts by setting a direction.

Management develops capacity by organizing and staffing.

Leadership develops capacity by aligning people.

Management achieves by controlling and problem solving.

Leadership achieves by motivating and inspiring.

THE MYTH OF THE GREAT LEADER (USUALLY A MAN)

This epithet Great Man Theory was first described by Thomas Carlyle in his book On Heroes, Hero-Workshop, and the Heroic in History.[7] He wrote,

> *Universal History, the history of what man has accomplished in this world, is at bottom the History of the Great Men who have worked here. They were the leaders of men, these great ones; the modellers, patterns, and in a wide sense creators, of whatsoever the general mass of men contrived to do or to attain; all things that we see standing accomplished*

in the world are properly the outer material result, the practical realization and embodiment of thoughts that dwelt in the Great Men sent into the world: the soul of the whole world's history, it may justly be considered, were the history of these.

We are all familiar as to who this title refers to: Julius Caesar, Napoleon, Churchill, Mussolini and Hitler. And of course we could include Jesus Christ, Mohamed and Attila the Hun.

Albert Einstein

Franklin D. Roosevelt

Julius Caesar

William Shakespeare

Critiques of this theory include Henry Spencer, the philosopher. Hegel wrote,

The goal of humanity lies in its highest specimens. [8]

Although he later disagreed with Carlyle's notion of the "Hero Cult" in *Ecce Homo*.[9]

The big debate continues as to whether the Great Man chooses the cause or whether the "tribe", the "country" or the "time" chooses the man.

We can appreciate the complexity of the debate as we ponder on whether both Biden and Trump are examples of the Great Man Theory.

What I believe we can accept is that the epithet is linked to supposed success, either in battle (Caesar), in discovery (Einstein), in literature (Shakespeare) or in politics (Roosevelt).

In his book *The Evolution of Everything* [10] Matt Ridley addressed the evolution of leadership and uses the example of "tackling poverty". He writes,

> *Giving money to poor people is not a sustainable solution to poverty. So how do you help poor people? Do you instruct, plan and order their lives with expertise and lots of government or do you get them freedom to exchange and specialise, so that prosperity can evolve?* [11]

He quotes,

> *Bell Condliffe, saw what was happening, and warned presciently in 1938: 'We face a new and more formidable superstition than the world has ever known: the myth of the nation-state, whose priests are as intolerant as those of the Inquisition.' Condliffe saw autocratic power as the cause of, not the solution to, poverty.* [12]

He makes his own positon clear.

> *Today we are still in thrall to Great Man history, if only because we like reading biography. American presidential politics is entirely based on the myth that a perfect, omniscient, virtuous and incorruptible saviour will emerge from the New Hampshire primary every four years, and proceed to lead his people to the promised land. Never was the mesianic mood more extreme than on the day Barack Obama won the presidency. This was the moment, he himself has said in June 2008, when 'the rise of the oceans began to slow and our planet began to heal'. He was going to 'heal the nation', close Guantanamo Bay, reform healthcare,*

bring peace to the Middle East. He was given the Nobel Peace Prize simply for having been elected. Amid such expectations he could not, poor chap, fail to disappoint. [13]

You will have noticed that this previous section on the "Great Man Theory" nowhere examines the "feminine", or indeed the model of women as world leaders. As yet there has been no mention of the attributes and skills that need to exist in the concept of compassionate leadership. It is to this aspect of leadership that we must now explore.

UNDER MY LEADERSHIP

I must take all that
Are here and I must
Do what is there to do
And must know what
To refrain from.

And who am I
what is there to do
I must know here
At this moment,
I must keep
My understanding
Strong and I must
Distinguished from bad and good.

Gajanan Mishra [14]

ATTRIBUTES OF THE COMPASSIONATE LEADER

In one of the major studies by Harvard Business School [15] on what attributes can be identified in "great leaders", the following four appear to be consistently present: cognitive skills, technical skills, IQ and emotional intelligence. When the ratio between these four major attributes were calculated it was apparent that emotional intelligence was twice as important a factor as the first three (not that these were not important as well).

What is emotional intelligence?

In his book *On Leadership* [16] Goleman outlines his own definition of what he understands by the term "emotional intelligence":

It is noticeable that there is no mention of compassion in the index – as indeed, the word compassion appears nowhere in Charles Darwin's work.

Understanding EI's Components

EI Component	Definition	Hallmarks	Example
Self-awareness	Knowing one's emotions, strengths, weakness, drives, values, and goals—and their impact on others	• Self-confidence • Realistic self-assessment • Self-deprecating sense of humor • Thirst for constructive critic	A manager knows tight deadlines bring out the worst in him. So he plans his time to get work done well in advance
Self-regulation	Controlling or redirecting disruptive emotions and impulses	• Trustworthiness • Integrity • Comfort with ambiguity and change	When a team botches a presentation, its leader resists the urge to scream. Instead, she considers possible reasons for the failure, explains the consequences to her team, and explores solutions with them
Motivation	Being driven to achieve for the sake of achievement	• A passion for the work itself and for new challenges • Unflagging energy to improve • Optimism in the face of failure	A portfolio manager at an investment company sees his fund tumble for three consecutive quarters. Major clients defect. Instead of blaming external circumstances, she decides to learn from the experience—and engineers a turn-around.
Empathy	Considering others' feelings, especially when making decisions	• Expertise in attracting and retaining talent • Ability to develop others • Sensitivity to cross-cultural differences	An American consultant and her team pitch a project to a potential client in Japan. Her team interprets the client's silence as disapproval, and prepares to leave. The consultant reads the client's body language and senses Interest. She continues the meeting and her team gets the job
Social skills	Managing relationships to move people in desired directions	• Effectiveness in leading change • Persuasiveness • Extensive networking • Expertise in building and leading teams	A manager wants his company to adopt a better internet strategy. He finds kindred spirits and assembles a de facto team to crate a prototype website. He persuades allies in other divisions to fund the company's participation in a relevant convention. His company forms an internet division and puts him in charge of it.

What would Charles Darwin have to say about compassion?

Darwin's theory of evolution by natural selection is the corner-stone of our modern understanding of both human and non-human origins and development. In his three major works: *On the Origin of Species*, [17] *The Expression of the Emotions in Man and Animals* [18] and *The Descent of Man*, [19] it is possible to trace his understanding of the evolutionary nature of compassion and empathy, although he refers to these qualities in terms of "sympathy", "moral actions" and "social instinct" in keeping with the then contemporary parlance. Darwin's treatises, while complex and exploratory, do not reflect the glib shorthand of "survival of the fittest" that has since become commonplace.

Instead, Darwin's position appears to reject the supremacy of crass self-interest, focusing instead on a range of human emotions, including sympathy for others, including those beyond our family group or species. In *The Descent of Man*, he wrote:

> *We are ... impelled to relieve the sufferings of another, in order that our own painful feelings may be at the same time relieved. In like manner we are led to participate in the pleasures of others*[20]

In short, Darwin's research suggests that humans have evolved to behave compassionately or, at least, that we have the capacity to do so. Recent discoveries in neuroscience and neural-imaging support this biological basis for compassion, but it was Darwin who originally argued that

> *[T]hose communities which contained the greatest number of the most sympathetic members would flourish best, and rear the greatest number of offspring.* [21]

Modern Darwinism shows how humans are intimately related to all other organisms on our planet, a cognitive-emotional tonic for improved biophilia as well as kinder, more inclusive relations between human beings. Humans derive a sense of meaning from performing costly prosocial altruistic acts, and happiness from receiving such kindnesses from others. The brain has developed in a way that allows us to engage in complex indirect and time-delayed reciprocity. We can experience the positive emotions associated with compassionate action without being immediately repaid by the same individuals we help – these positive emotions breed happiness and more compassionate action.

Sympathy beyond the confines of man, that is, humanity to the lower animals, seems to be one of the latest moral acquisitions…. This virtue, one of the noblest with which man is endowed, seems to arise incidentally from our sympathies becoming more tender and more widely diffused, until they are extended to all sentient beings. [22]

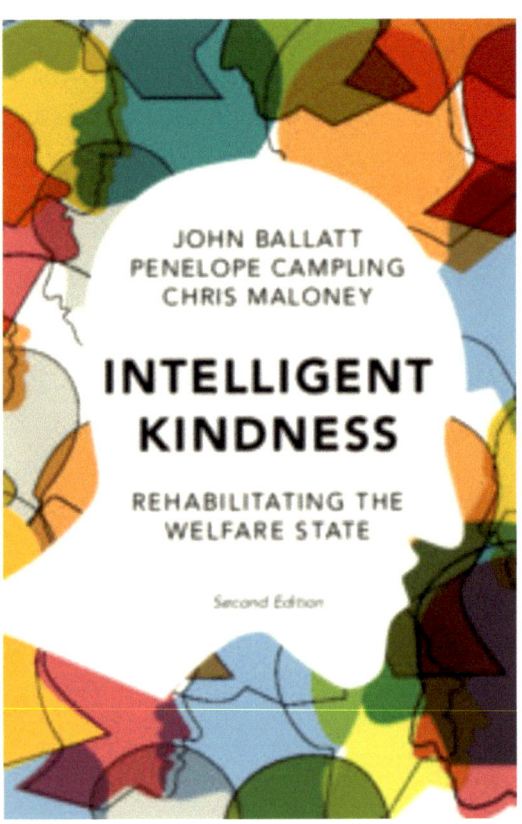

JOHN BALLATT
PENELOPE CAMPLING
CHRIS MALONEY

INTELLIGENT
KINDNESS

REHABILITATING THE
WELFARE STATE

Second Edition

The increasing awareness and understanding of the influence of "emotional intelligence" has propelled many others to explore and interrogate this concept (what I believe to be essential to the concept of compassion). My colleague, John Ballatt and Dr. Penny Campling's book *Intelligent Kindness: Reforming the Culture of Healthcare* [23] outlines in great detail how intelligent kindness is required to help reform the culture of Healthcare. I have drawn from the work of others to illustrate their understanding of what I will now label Compassionate Leadership:

> *The process of becoming a leader is much the same as becoming an integrated human being.*
> Warren Bennis & Burt Nanus [24]

> *If your organisation has only one leader, then it is almost certainly short of leadership.*
> Gerard Egan [25]

> *Leadership requires us to be psychologically present and personally engaged with the authenticity of working with one's real emotions.*
> Francesca Cardona [26]

> *The capacity to generate and sustain trust is the central ingredient in leadership.*
> Benna & Nanus [27]

Compassionate leaders use five key skills:

- The ability to accept people as they are, not as you would like them to be
- The capacity to approach relationships in terms of the present rather than the past
- The ability to treat those who are close to you with the same courteous attention that you extend to strangers and casual acquaintances
- The ability to trust others even if the risk seems great
- The ability to do without constant approval and recognition from others (pp 52-63) [28]

LEADERSHIP CRISIS

An acute shortage of sound leadership
An acute shortage of wise leadership
An acute shortage of visionary leadership
An acute shortage of self less leadership
An acute shortage of integrity in leaders
An acute shortage of humility in leaders
A leadership crisis in the world.

Ideal leadership long ceased to exist
The moral compass in leadership nonexistent
The leaders themselves need to be led
The blind in essence are leading the blind
The leaders are struggling to lead
A leadership crisis in the world.

Hypocrites leading the world
Arrogant men leading the world
Corrupt men leading the world
Evil men leading the world
Way ward men leading the world
Proud men leading the world
Self important men leading the world
A leadership crisis in the world.

Qiniso Mogale [29]

As a result of much of the work described above, several authors have begun to adopt different labels to accommodate the necessity for emotional intelligence, eg:

Stewardship
Adaptive Leadership
Servant Leadership

I use the term *compassionate leadership* but draw on all three other models of leadership. I outline briefly these different titles.

STEWARD AND STEWARDSHIP

JOHN WESLEY'S RULE OF LIFE

Do all the good you can,
By all the means you can,
In all the ways you can,
In all the places you can,
At all the times you can,
To all the people you can,
As long as ever you can.

Attributed to Reverend John Wesley [30]

Steward is a 12th Century old English word used to describe someone employed to "manage" or "look after" a large household. *Stewardship* has many theological and religious meanings, and links to the Bible and the concept of the good shepherd. *Steward and Stewardship* is now in common use referring to environmental concerns and responsible use and protection of the natural environment through conservation and sustainable practices (Merriam Webster Dictionary). The concept of stewardship applied to higher education offers a way of understanding the entrepreneurial nature of universities, and in particular, the relationship between education and health in relation to the development and "wellness" of communities. [31]

Professor Mike Thomas, when Vice-Chancellor of the University of Central Lancashire, highlighted the challenges faced by organisational leaders who have the desire to influence changes within large organisations. He wrote in a recent article in the *Higher Education Supplement* entitled "Heroic Leadership is a Campus Villain". [32]

Universities are not capitalist enterprises, and leaders forget this at their peril. Business models purloined from the private sector will always be an uneasy fit. We occupy a distinctive position in society, straddling elements of the private, public and charitable spheres.

So rather than the heroic model, I'm an advocate of the "stewardship model". University leaders are "keepers of the flame", custodians of institutions that are more important than any one individual. During our tenure, we are charged with ensuring that our institutions continue to succeed in their remits to offer people the life-changing benefits of higher education and enable them to achieve their potential. These values are important because they provide the foundation of our activities.

ADAPTIVE LEADERSHIP

Adaptive leadership draws heavily on Darwin's theory of evolution – remember that he never wrote "the survival of the fittest". Darwin believed that those who could adapt to changing circumstances would survive.

When an organization tries to adapt, it steps out of its familiar mode of existence that has worked so far, much as a plant or animal species does by random mutation. The new mode may help or hinder an organization – or an organism's progeny. Not all adaptions work in the long run. Some survive and thrive; many fail, and many organizations and species die off.

Ronald Heifetz and Marty Linsky are co-founders and Alexander Grashow is managing director of the Cambridge Leadership Associates. This section is based on their book *The Practice of Adaptive Leadership*, recently published by Harvard Business Press.

Your challenge, as you adapt to meet the future, is to make the best possible use of the wisdom your organization has acquired. Do so by engaging your people in the arduous task of examining all that you value, separating out what is essential and leaving behind what no longer works.

Similarly, after more than 200 years, the U.S. still has a structure of governance, values and a way of life that closely reflect those of the Founding Fathers. The Constitution has been tweaked but not radically changed. Southwest Airlines does only a few distinct things differently from other airlines, yet it has been profitable for 36 straight years in a treacherous industry.

Every adaptation involves giving something up, some part of the DNA that the species or the organization relied on in the past. You cannot make progress if you can't learn to sacrifice something in order to adapt to the unknown future.

What is called Adaptive Leadership was developed by members of the faculty at Harvard University and has been refined by more than 30 years of practical application at corporations all over the world. It draws on Darwin and the work of evolutionary biologists to understand how corporations can act to survive and thrive in rapidly changing environments and conditions of great uncertainty. [33]

We need only draw on our own experience of the impact of Covid – not only on the many individuals who have died, but on all the small businesses, big corporations, airlines, etc. who have been unable to adapt to the devastating impact of a very small virus. We can also fairly judge our leaders by how they have ensured that both individuals and organisations have been supported enough to be able to survive.

SERVANT LEADERSHIP

The concept of servant leadership was first proposed by Robert K. Greenleaf in his article *"The Servant as Leader"* [34] published in 1970. It could be summarised as follows:

> *I serve because I am the Leader.*

> *I am the Leader because I serve.*

Greenleaf emphasised what others went on to call *Emotional Intelligence*. It is in his description of what he understands to be *Servant Leadership* that we come across the words altruism, compassion, authentic and transformative leadership.

Greenleaf was heavily influenced by reading Herman Hesse's book *Journey to the East* [35] (1932), and would have agreed with the Dalai Lama's statement,

> *Love and compassion are necessities, not luxuries.*
> *Without them, humanity would not survive.* [36]

Research into the concept of Servant Leadership has produced a list of attributes as well as attempts to create scales and questionnaires to measure the practice of Servant Leadership. Below are some examples, but I would approach this tendency to measure the unmeasurable with caution. *Statistics are a fine thing because they allow us to stop thinking (and feeling).*

Larry Spears – Ten Characteristics of Servant Leadership

Empathy; listening; healing; awareness; persuasion; conceptualisation; foresight; stewardship; commitment to the growth of people and building community.

Jo Larocci in his book *Servant Leadership in the Workplace* [37] identifies the following:

3 Key Priorities: Developing people, building a trusting team and achieving results
3 Key Principles: Serve first, persuasion, empowerment
3 Key Practices: Listening, delegating, connecting followers to the mission

Further, researchers have developed scales to measure:

Altruistic calling
Emotional healing
Wisdom
Persuasive mapping
Organisational stewardship

Even more ambitious attempts have been made to identify a leader's spiritual dimension. This links back to Greenleaf's original model based on the influence Hesse's book *Journey to the East* [38] had on his original description.

How does the concept of compassion fit into these models of leadership I have outlined?

The Great Man Theory/Steward and Stewardship
Adaptive Leadership/Servant Leadership

I can do no better than to draw your attention to the current leadership styles offered by the two candidates for the Presidency of the United States – Donald Trump and Joe Biden.

Can I suggest you use the following list of leadership attributes and mark them on a scale of 1 to 5: 1 = weak and 5 = strong.

Leadership Attributes	TRUMP	BIDEN
Top Down		
Bottom Up		
Visionary		
Builder		
Transformer		
Commander		
Decision Maker		
Master		
"Great Man"		
Emotional Intelligence		
Self Awareness		
Self Regulation		
Motivation		
Empathy		
Social Skills		
Intelligent Kindness		
Trusting		
Integrated Human Being		
Stewardship		
Adaptive Leadership		
Servant Leadership		
Listening		
Delegation		
Wisdom		
Foresight		
Building Communities		
Compassion		

Scales 1 (low) to 5 (high)

CONCLUSION

I conclude this series of ten volumes by republishing the Position Paper written by my colleagues John Ballatt and Laura Noszlopy. We circulated this paper following the launch Conference of the Darwin International Institute for the Study of Compassion in 2015.

The Darwin International Institute for the Study of Compassion
A Position Paper

Introduction

It is proposed that an academic Institute be established to explore, learn about, teach, and promote compassion as a core value and practice in personal, professional, organisational, social, inter-communal and international relations.

Easily championed, but everywhere alarmingly challenged, compassion can too readily be relegated to a "soft" or "pious" quality, sidelined by more instrumental, technical, pragmatic or ideological concerns. Compassion needs to be re-considered, re-evaluated and integrated into the understanding and practices of society as:

- a primary value and requirement in a modern world that, at individual, social, institutional and political levels, frequently fosters its opposite – to the extent that fear of annihilation, of valued social institutions, of groups, and of the self – is widespread;

- treating the other(s) with the same concern, attention and generosity that one would wish for oneself; refraining from treating them as one would not wish for oneself; being open to, disturbed by, sympathetic to, and moved to respond to the experience and pain of others;

- a difficult and challenging quality that itself requires better understanding; which also requires the recognition of, and engagement with, pain, damage, anxiety, anger and difference, and the exploitative, competitive, violent or simply self-centred feelings and motives by which human beings, individually and collectively, are also driven;

- something that has been split off from and relegated to a subsidiary place in technical or professional skills, and collective enterprises, and that needs to be reintegrated as a core and primary component of all such practices and wider social relations;

- an evolutionary phenomenon emerging as a positive and dynamic aspect in social relations as human beings have learned to cooperate and preserve themselves and their communities;

- an attitude and a practice that, in turn, depends on social relations for its cultivation and sustenance – relations that can be thought about, constructed and nourished to do that, or which can work directly against compassionate mindedness and behaviour;

- a quality that depends on the individual, the group, the organisation and society developing the skills and the habit of self-awareness and reflection;

- a quality that requires, for its exploration and understanding, a meeting of, dialogue between and synthesis of many traditions and discourses, including scientific, psychological, philosophical, historical, cultural, religious, sociological and political perspectives.

The Work of the Institute

The Institute will make the development and support of the young, especially future leaders, but whatever their roles, as intelligent and skilled promoters and sustainers of compassion, its core mission. The Institute will have four primary aims and functions

1. To stimulate and organize exploration, research, learning and education in and between a wide range of discourses and practices, as they help us understand compassion at individual, family, social, organisational, communal, inter-cultural and international levels.
2. To bring together these perspectives into dialogue, and mutual learning – promoting inter-disciplinary collaboration and common purpose
3. To understand the implications for all aspects of community life, such as education, health care, business, social policy, inter-cultural relations, etc.
4. To explore, develop and evaluate practices at any or all these levels and domains of life that promote and sustain compassion.

A more comprehensive picture of what this will involve might look like the following.

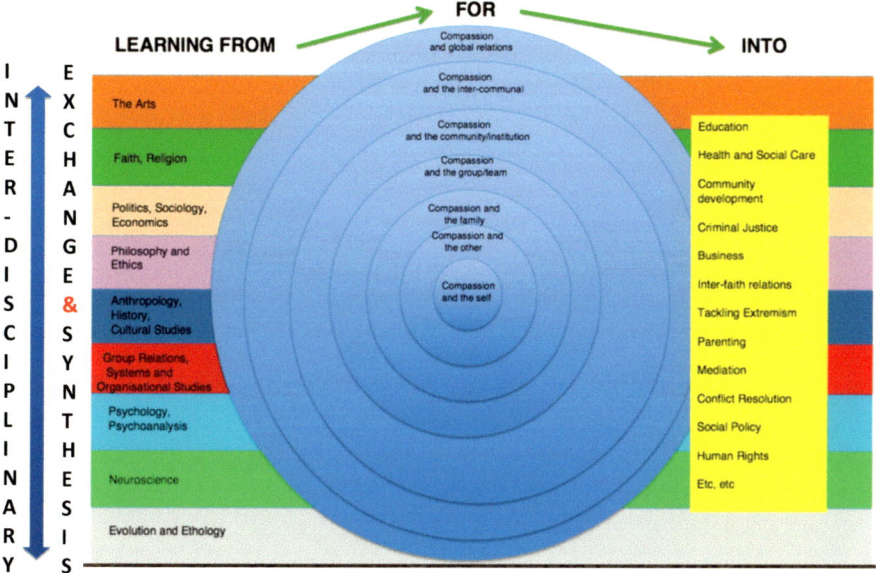

That perspective and concerns from different domains or disciplines will conflict or challenge each other is inevitable: the rule, though, will be that their exponents must agree to coexistence and dialogue. The Institute will model and promote Socratic dialogue, conversation and reflection – with a firm acceptance of the inevitability of doubt, and of the dark forces that can emerge within even the most benign of traditions and individuals.

Academic and exploratory consideration of compassion together will be part of 'changing the conversation', for individuals, and for the world of interaction, cooperation, organisation and society. The Institute will aim to develop fluency and credibility in working in such inter-disciplinary and inclusive ways and to encourage and develop an inclusive, academically credible and influential narrative about compassion.

The institute will involve five inter-related areas of activity

- Research
- Teaching
- "Social Criticism"
- Practice & Projects
- Dialogue and Influence

LEADERSHIP?

Who knows what leadership is?
I sometimes wonder
whether we should focus
more on followership.

Not just for those who follow,
but more importantly
for those who lead.

Can our leaders
learn to follow
from those willing to follow.
Listen carefully to their needs
and avoid their Privileged Ignorance;
and help identify
the Invisible Obvious.
How to lead with compassion.

Patrick Pietroni [39]

References

1. Pietroni, P. (2015). *Something Has to Change in Today's World! Let's Start with Future Leaders From Across the Globe. Huff Post.* Available at https://www.huffpost.com/entry/something-has-to-change-i_b_8220098?guccounter=1. Last accessed December 2020.

2. Keshavjee, M. (2018). Celebrating the launch of the a new Center for the Study of Compassion in the UK. *Ismaili Mail.* Available at Celebrating the launch of a new Centre for the Study of Compassion in the UK – Ismailimail. Last accessed December 2020.

3. Maswabi, K. (2015). *Leadership.* Available at www. poemhunter.com/ apoem/leadership-11/ Last accessed January 2021.

4. Rubenstein, D. M. (2020). *How to Lead.* Simon & Schuster.

5. Rubenstein, D. M. (2020). *ibid.*

6. Prince, J. (2009). *A Good Leadership.* Available at www.poem-hunter.com/poem/a-good-leadership/ Last accessed January 2021.

7. Carlyle, T. (1841). *On Heroes, Hero-Workshop, and the Heroic in History.* London. James Fraser.

8. Hegel, G. W. F. (1956. Originally published 1837). *Philosophy of History.* Trans. Sibree, J. New York. Dover.

9. Hegel, G. W. F. (1956. Originally published 1837). *ibid.*

10. Ridley, M. (2015). *The Evolution of Everything.* Fourth Estate.

11. Ridley, M. (2015). *ibid.*

12. Ridley, M. (2015). *op. cit.*

13. Ridley, M. (2015). *op. cit.*

14. Mishra, G. (2014). *Under My Leadership.* Available at www.poemhunter.com/poem/under-my-signature/#content. Last accessed January 2021.

15. Goleman, D. (2011). *On Leadership.* Harvard Business Review Press.

16. Goleman, D. (2011). *ibid.*

17. Darwin, C. (2004. First published 1859). *The Origin of Species by means of Natural Selection or the Preservation of Favoured Races in the Struggle for Life*. London. Castle Books.

18. Darwin, C. (1872). *The Expression of the Emotions in Man and Animals.* London. John Murray.

19. Darwin, C. (1871). *The Descent of Man* and *Selection in Relation to Sex*. London. John Murray.

20. Darwin, C. (1871). *ibid.*

21. Darwin, C. (1871). *op. cit.*

22. Darwin, C. (1871). *op. cit.*

23. Ballatt, J., Campling, P. & Maloney, C. (2020). *Intelligent Kindness: Rehabilitating the Welfare State.* Cambridge. Cambridge University Press.

24. Bennis, W. & Nanus, B. (2011). *Crucibles of Leadership.* Harvard Business Review. Press.

25. Egan, G. (2017)/ *The Skilled Helper: A problem-management and opportunity-development approach to helping.* Belmont. Brooks/Cole.

26. Cardona, F. (2002). The managers most precious skill. *Organisational & Social Dynamics*. November 2002: 226-235.

27. Bennis, W. & Nanus, B. (1997). *op. cit.*

28. Bennis, W. & Nanus, B. (1997). *op. cit.*

29. Mogale, Q. (2017). *Leadership Crisis*. Available at www.poemhunter.com/poem/leadership-crisis/. Last accessed January 2021.

30. Rev. Wesley, J. (1799). *John Wesley's Rule of Life*. Available at www.goodreads.com/quotes/12757-do-all-the-good-you-can-by-all-the-means. Last accessed January 2021.

31. Callejo Perez, D. M., & Ode, J. (Ed). (2013). *The Stewardship of Higher Education: Reimagining the Role of Education and Wellness on Community Impact.* Rotterdam, Sense Publishers.

32. Thomas, M. (2018). *Heroic Leadership is a Campus Villain.* Available at www.timeshighereducation.com/opinion/heroic-leadership-campus-villain. Last accessed January 2021.

33. Forbes (2009). *Management Advice from Charles Darwin.* Available at www.forbes.com/2009/06/25/darwin-natural-selection-leadership-managing-advice.html?sh=6e8907416b60. Last accessed January 2021.

34. Dittmar, J. K. (2006). An Interview with Larry Spears. *Journal of Leadership & Organizational Studies.* 13(1): 108-118.

35. Hesse, H. (2011. First published1932). *Journey to the East.* Martino Fine Books.

36. Ekman, P. (2014). *Moving towards global compassion.* Paul Ekman Group.

37. Larocci, J. (2017). *Servant Leadership in the Workplace.* Atlanta. Cairnway. Available at https://serveleadnow.com/ebook-servant-leadership-workplace-introduction/. Last accessed January 2021.

38. Hesse, H. (1932). *op. cit.*

39. Pietroni, P. (2021). *Leadership?* Unpublished.

Images

Image 1   Composite Image of Leaders. DIISC. Page 7.

Image 2   Leadership Wordcloud. DIISC. Page 9.

Image 3   Leadership Styles. Pietroni, P. (2014). After Croft, M. (1997). Page 10.

Image 4   Leadership compliments management. Kotter, J. (1990). What leaders really do. Harvard Business Review. Page 12.

Image 5   Composite Image of Myth of Great Leaders. DIISC. Page 13.

Image 6   Great Men composite. DIISC. Page 14.

Image 7   Barak Obama and Family - By Annie Leibovitz / Released by White House Photo Office - The Official White House Photostream [1], Public Domain, https://commons.wikimedia.org/w/index.php?curid=8224935   Page 15.

Image 8   Understanding EI's Components table. Goleman, D. (2011). *On Leadership*. Harvard Business Review Press. Page 19.

Image 9   Charles Darwin Statue, Shrewsbury. Lee Good. Page 20.

Image 10 *Intelligent Kindness: Rehabilitating the Welfare State*. Front cover. Page 22.

Image 11 Stewardship. Sam Barber on Unsplash. Page 26.

Image 12 Leadership Attributes. DIISC (2021). Page 33.

Image 13 Inter-disciplinary exchange & synthesis. DIISC. Page 37.

Image 14 DIISC Steering Group. DIISC. Page 38.

Image 1 Composite Image of Leaders:

Indra Nooyi. By JeffBedford from Arlington, Virginia, United States - posted to Flickr as Indra Nooyi, PepsiCo CEO, Speaking at the World Economic Forum 2010 Annual Meeting, CC BY-SA 2.0, https://commons.wikimedia.org/w/index.php?curid=12566849

Colin Powel. By Russell Roederer - http://www.dodmedia.osd.mil/, Public Domain, https://commons.wikimedia.org/w/index.php?curid=523224

Condeleezza Rice. By Department of State - https://2009-2017.state.gov/cms_images/newer2_8x10_500e.jpg, Public Domain, https://commons.wikimedia.org/w/index.php?curid=3160612

Ruth Bader Ginsburgh. By Simmie Knox, under commission of the United States Supreme Court - http://dcchs.org/usca/RuthGinsburg.jpg, Public Domain, https://commons.wikimedia.org/w/index.php?curid=23263923

Renee Fleming. By David Shankbone - David Shankbone, CC BY 3.0, https://commons.wikimedia.org/w/index.php?curid=7873682

Marilyn Hewson. By NASA - http://www.nasa.gov/press/2014/april/high-school-students-create-winning-design-for-nasas-first-flight-of-orion/#.VBiRFPldWyu, Public Domain, https://commons.wikimedia.org/w/index.php?curid=35419536

Bill and Melinda Gates. By Kjetil Ree - Own work, CC BY-SA 3.0, https://commons.wikimedia.org/w/index.php?curid=6934215

Richard Branson. By User:David Shankbone -
David Shankbone, CC BY 3.0, https://commons.wikimedia.org/w/
index.php?curid=10269869

Barak Obama. By Official White House Photo by Pete Souza
P120612PS-0463 (direct link)https://web.archive.org/web/
20160227060205/https://www.whitehouse.gov/administra-
tion/president-obama (Official White House page - direct
link), Public Domain,
https://commons.wikimedia.org/w/index.php?curid=23956389

Image 5 Composite Image of Myth of Great Leaders:
Mohammed. By Unknown author -
http://www.zombietime.com/mohammed_image_archive/
islamic_mo_full/, Public Domain, https://commons.wikimedia.org/w/
index.php?curid=12046943

Attila the Hun. By Eugène Delacroix - Web Gallery of Art:
Public Domain, https://commons.wikimedia.org/w/
index.php?curid=5965258

Benito Mussolini. By http://www.ilduce.net/foto-benito-musso-
lini/43-2/ This file was derived from: Benito Mussolini (primo
piano). Public Domain, https://commons.wikimedia.org/w/
index.php?curid=64572838

Julius Caesar. By Lionel Royer - Musée CROZATIER du
Puy-en-Velay. — http://www.mairie-le-puy-en-velay.fr.http://
forum.artinvestment.ru/blog.php?b=273473&langid=5,
Public Domain, https://commons.wikimedia.org/w/
index.php?curid=1218850

Napoleon Bonaparte. By Jacques-Louis David - Google Art Project, Public Domain, https://commons.wikimedia.org/w/index.php?curid=38872895

Winston Churchill. By digitized by: BiblioArchives / Library Archives - Flickr: Sir Winston Churchill, Public Domain, https://commons.wikimedia.org/w/index.php?curid=41991931

Jesus Christ. By José Ferraz de Almeida Júnior - artsandculture.google.com, Public Domain, https://commons.wikimedia.org/w/index.php?curid=78290933

Adolf Hitler. By Bundesarchiv, Bild 183-H1216-0500-002 / CC-BY-SA, CC BY-SA 3.0 de, https://commons.wikimedia.org/w/index.php?curid=5780403

Image 6 Great Men composite:
Julius Caesar. Public Domain, https://commons.wikimedia.org/w/index.php?curid=91281949

Franklin D. Roosevelt. By Vincenzo Laviosa - iQHA8LCrsSxF4Q sur l'Institut culturel Google résolution maximale, Public Domain, https://commons.wikimedia.org/w/index.php?curid=22652911

Albert Einstein. By Ferdinand Schmutzer - http://www.bhm.ch/de/news_04a.cfm?bid=4&jahr=2006 [dead link], archived copy (image), Public Domain, https://commons.wikimedia.org/w/index.php?curid=34239518

William Shakespeare. By John Taylor - Official gallery link, Public Domain, https://commons.wikimedia.org/w/index.php?curid=5442977

Publisher
SF Design, llc / Fresco Books
Albuquerque, New Mexico
frescobooks.com

ISBN: 978-1-934491-83-6